English Code 4

Phonics Book

International Phonetic Alphabet (IPA)

IPA SYMBOLS

Consonants

/b/	bag, bike
/d/	desk, opened
/f/	face, free, laugh, photo
/g/	game, good
/h/	hit, hot
/k/	key, kite
/l/	lamp, lucky
/m/	man, monkey
/n/	neck, nut
/ŋ/	ring, flying
/p/	pen, pink
/r/	run, rock
/s/	sun, sell, cycle, grapes
/ʃ/	shirt, shut, shell
/t/	tent, knocked
/θ/	thick, thirsty
/ð/	this, there
/v/	visit, give
/w/	wall, window, what
/ks/	relax, taxi
/j/	yellow, young
/z/	zoo, bananas
/tʃ/	chair, cheese, cheap
/dʒ/	jeans, juice, judge, ginger

Two-Letter Consonant Blend

/bl/	blanket, blue
/pl/	plane, planet
/kl/	clean, climb
/gl/	glass, glove
/fl/	fly, floor
/sl/	sleep, slow
/br/	break, branch
/pr/	price, practice
/kr/	crab
/fr/	fruit
/gr/	grass
/dr/	draw
/tr/	train
/ŋk/	bank, think
/nd/	stand, round
/nt/	student, count
/sk/	scarf, skirt, basket, scary
/sm/	small
/sn/	snow
/sp/	sports, space
/st/	stand, first, stay
/sw/	swim, sweet
/tw/	twelve, twins
/kw/	quick, question

Three-Letter Consonant Blend

/spr/	spring
/str/	street
/skr/	screen
/skw/	square

Vowels

🇺🇸 /ɑː/ 🇬🇧 /ɒ/	top, jog, wash
/æ/	cat, clap, sand
/e/	wet, send, healthy
/ɪ/	hit, sing, pin
/ɔː/	caught, saw, cough
🇺🇸 /ɔːr/ 🇬🇧 /ɔː/	horse, morning
/eɪ/	cake, name, say
/iː/	eat, tree, steam
🇺🇸 /oʊ/ 🇬🇧 /əʊ/	home, coat, snow
/uː/	food, glue, flew, June
/ʌ/	duck, run, cut, honey
/ʊ/	cook, foot, put
🇺🇸 /ər/ 🇬🇧 /ə/	ruler, teacher
/ɜːr/	bird, hurt, word, learn

Diphthongs

/aɪ/	nice, bike
/aʊ/	house, brown
/ɔɪ/	boil, enjoy
🇺🇸 /aːr/ 🇬🇧 /aː/	card, market
🇺🇸 /aɪr/ 🇬🇧 /aɪə/	fire, hire
🇺🇸 /aʊr/, /aʊər/ 🇬🇧 /aʊər/	hour, flower
🇺🇸 /er/ 🇬🇧 /eə/	chair, bear, there
🇺🇸 /ɪr/ 🇬🇧 /ɪə/	near, engineer
/juː/	cute, huge, few

Vowel and Consonant Blend

/ʃən/	station, dictionary
/ɪz/	beaches, bridges
/ɪd/	visited

Contents

1 ir / ear

1 02 **Listen, point, and repeat.**

ir

1

bird

2

ear

learn

3

shirt

4

search

5

thirty

6

early

2 🎧 💬 Listen. Then say.

The thirsty bird arrived early
To search for food and a drink.
He tapped three times on my window
To wake me up early, I think.
I gave him a dish of water.
He said, "Thank you!"
And gave me a wink.

3 🎭 Act out the rhyme.

2 air / ear

1 🎧 04 Listen, point, and repeat.

air

1

ch**air**

3

h**air**

5

f**air**

ear

2

b**ear**

4

p**ear**

6

w**ear**

2  **Listen. Then say.**

I wish I could visit the fair,
Take a ride on a swing with a bear,
Way up in the clear blue air,
Feel the wind on my face and hair,
Then enjoy a delicious pear.
I'd be so happy way up there.

Ferris Wheel

3 **Imagine you are at the fair in 2. Draw a picture. Then show a partner and say the rhyme together.**

3  ear / eer

1 Listen, point, and repeat.

ear

1
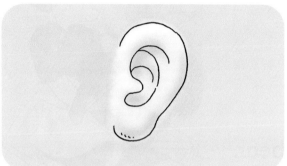
ear

3

near

5

year

eer

2

engineer

4

cheer

6

deer

2  Listen and read.

🇺🇸 American · 🇬🇧 British
Grandma · Granny

Dear Grandma,
It's getting very near to
New Year. So I'm sending you
a letter to cheer you up. See
you on New Year's Day.

Love from
Vera

3 Think of someone dear to you. Write another letter.

Review 1

1 Play the game. Listen and draw the route. Then say the words.

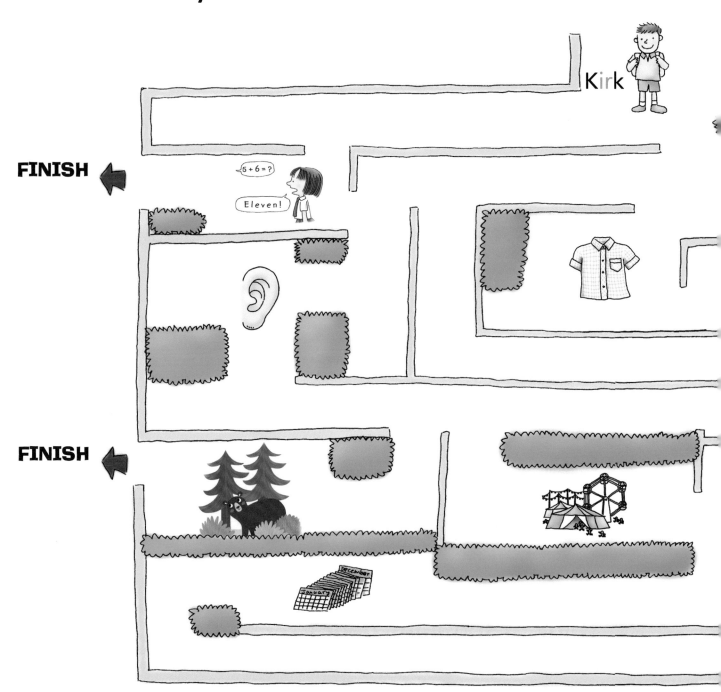

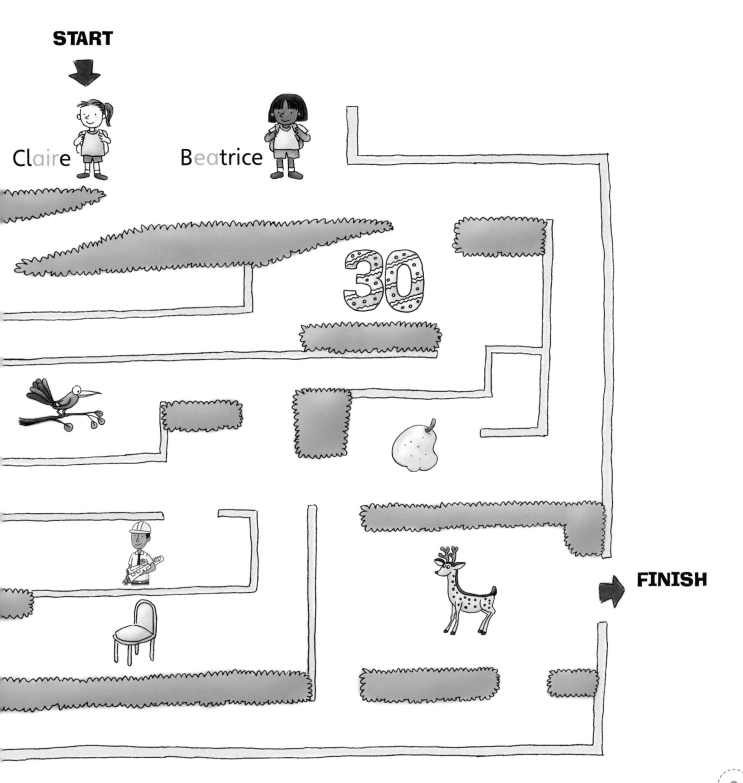

START

Claire   Beatrice

FINISH

4

bl **pl**

1  Listen, point, and repeat.

bl

1

bl**anket**

2

block

3

bl**ue**

pl

4

plane

5

plate

6

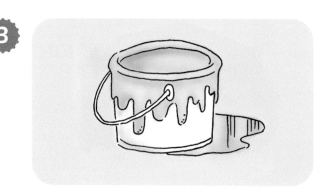

planet

2  Listen. Then sing.

🇺🇸 American | 🇬🇧 British

soccer | football

My soccer team wears black and blue,
Black and blue.
My soccer team wears black and blue,
Black and blue.
See them play, hear me cheer.
We will get first place this year.
My soccer team wears black and blue.

3 Design a uniform for a soccer team.

4   cl   gl

4 🎧 **Listen, point, and repeat.**

cl

1

clean

4

glass

2

climb

5

glue

3

clock

6

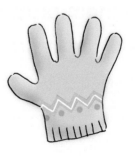

glove

gl

5 🔧 💬 Listen and read.

May 3

Yesterday, I forgot to wear my glasses.

I couldn't see the clock clearly.

I was late for class.

May 4

I'm glad I have my glasses on today.

6 💬 What else did the boy forget?

He forgot ...

4 · fl · sl

7 🎧 14 **Listen, point, and repeat.**

fl

1

fly

2
floor

3

flower

sl

4

sleep

5
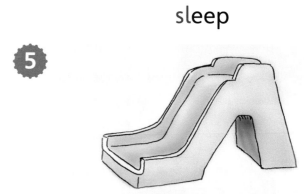
slide

6

slow

8 🎧 💬 Listen and read.

1 I am learning to ski.
Slowly I stand up.

2 Now I can slide down.

3 I slide faster and faster …
I can almost fly.

4 Oh, no! It's very slippery.
I fall flat on the floor!

9 🎨 Act out the story.

5

 **br**

 pr

1 Listen, point, and repeat.

 br

pr

1

break

4

prize

2

brown

5

$15

price

3

branch

6

practice

2  Listen and read.

🇺🇸 American	🇬🇧 British
hall monitor	prefect

My brother is a hall monitor at school. He is bright and brave.

He has soccer practice every day and hopes to win the first prize again.

Everybody praises my brother. I'm really proud of him.

3 Act out the story.

17

5

cr **fr** **gr**

4 🎧18 Listen, point, and repeat.

cr **1**

crab

2

cry

fr **3**

fridge

4

fruit

gr **5**

grass

6

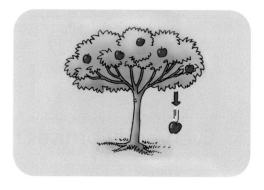

gravity

5 Listen and read.

Don't cry!
If you eat too much ice cream,
You will get sick.
But if you eat fresh green fruit,
You will grow taller than the fridge.

I like ...

6 Draw a list of the fruits you like and tell the class.

5

dr **tr**

7 Listen, point, and repeat.

dr

1

draw

2

drink

3

drama

tr

4

train

5
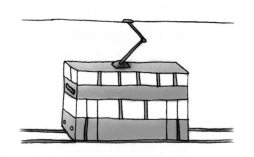
tram

6

tree

8  Listen and read.

I dream about driving a car. I dream about making a trip to the park. I can take lots of food and drink.

If the weather is hot and dry, I can stop driving and have a picnic under a tree.

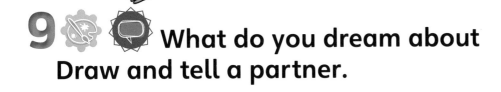

9 What do you dream about Draw and tell a partner.

Review 2

1 🎧 22 Listen and say the words.

1

block
clock

2

bridge
fridge

3

cream
green

4

drain
train

5

drawer
floor

6

prize
fries

7

glass
grass

8

glide
slide

9

plane
train

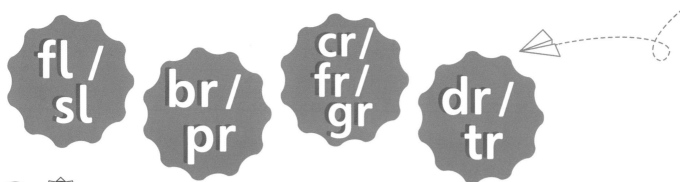

2 Choose and write nine words. Play *Bingo*.

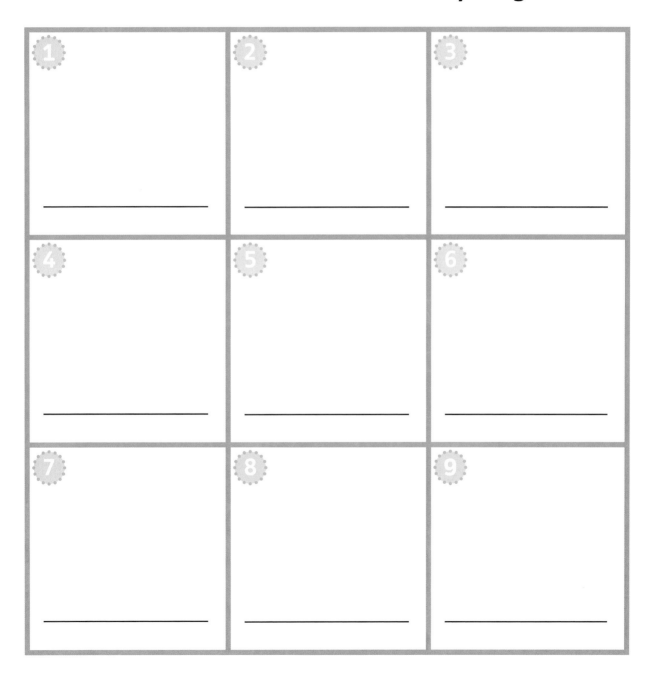

6 sc / sk

1 🎧 Listen, point, and repeat.

sc

1

scarf

3

score

5

scout

sk

2

skate

4

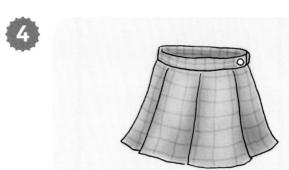

skirt

6

sky

2  ♪ Listen. Then sing.

Put down your school bag,
Take off your scarf.
Put on your skates,
Let's go to the park.
We can play, we can laugh,
We can skate in the sun.
Put down your school bag,
Take off your scarf.

3 Act out the song.

6 sm sn

4 🎧 Listen, point, and repeat.

sm

1

small

2

smell

3

smooth

sn

4

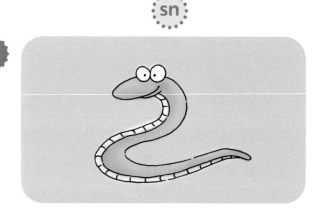

snake

5

snore

6

snow

5  Listen. Then say.

Can you see the small brown snake,
Sleeping in the sun?
Can you see its smooth long shape,
Sleeping in the sun?
Can you hear the snake snoring,
Sleeping in the sun?

6 Draw a house in the country. Add as many things as you can starting with s.

6 sp st

7  Listen, point, and repeat.

sp

1

sp**eak**

2

sp**ell**

3

sp**orts**

st

4

st**and**

5

st**ar**

6

st**op**

8  **Listen. Then say.**

At night, if you stop and stand very still,
Take a look around up high.
You'll see millions of special stars,
Little spots of light in the sky.

Your stars look like …

9 **Draw your own group of stars in the sky. Ask a partner to say what they look like.**

6 SW

10 🎧 Listen, point, and repeat.

1

sw**an**

2

sw**eat**

3

sw**eep**

4

sw**eet**

5

sw**im**

6

sw**ing**

11 Listen and read.

I can swim like a swan.

I can swing in the trees like a monkey.

I can sing a sweet song like a bird.

But I have to sweep the floor!

12 Act out the story.

Review 3

sc / sk

1 🔧 32 💬 **Play the game. Say words for the pictures. Say words with the letters.**

START

sm

climb

c-l-i-m-b

st

TEAM A TEAM B

3 2

sw

sp

sn

sk

sc

sm/ sn

sp/ st

sw

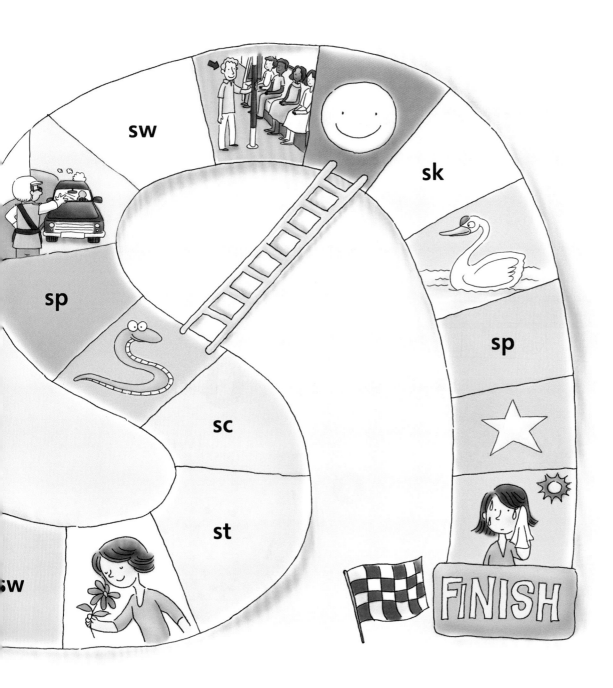

sw

sk

sp

sw

sp

sc

st

sw

FINISH

7 tw

1 🎧 33 Listen, point, and repeat.

1

twelfth

2

twelve

3

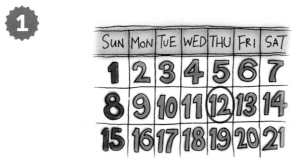

twice

4

twins

5

twist

6

twenty

2 🎧 💬 Listen. Then say.

Twelve ladies are on the dance floor.
The twelfth lady has a twin sister.
Do you think the twins will have twice as much fun?

3 ✏️ Draw an outfit for a dance party.

7  qu

4 🎧 35 Listen, point, and repeat.

1

qu**een**

2

qu**ick**

3

qu**iet**

4

qu**iz**

5

qu**arter**

6

What's your name?

qu**estion**

5 Listen. Then say.

Now the last question. Where's the Taj Mahal?

It's fun to watch a TV quiz.

It's always a surprise.

If you answer questions quickly,

You may get the winning prize.

6 Write a quiz question for a partner to answer.

The answer is ...

8 c g j

| 🇺🇸 American |
| center |
| 🇬🇧 British |
| centre |

1 🎧 37 Listen, point, and repeat.

c

1

center

2
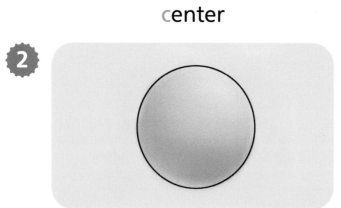
circle

3

cycle

g j

4

bandage

5

judge

6

ginger

2 🔁³⁸ 💬 Listen. Then say.

The park in the city center is large.
It has a huge bridge.
You can run. You can jog.
But you can't cycle.
It's a pity there's no cycle path.

3 💬 Is there a park near your school? What is there in the park?

...

Review 4

1 Play the game. Say words for the pictures. Say rhyming words.

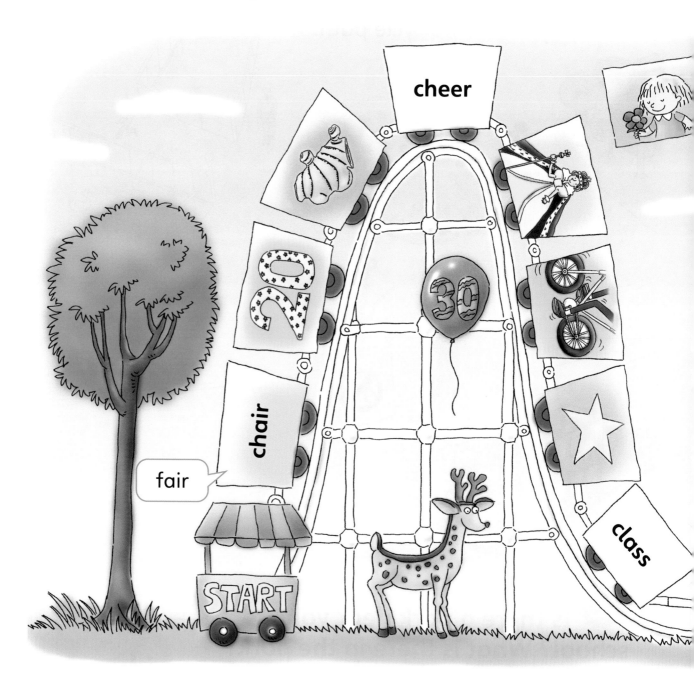

cheer

chair

fair

START

class

more ...

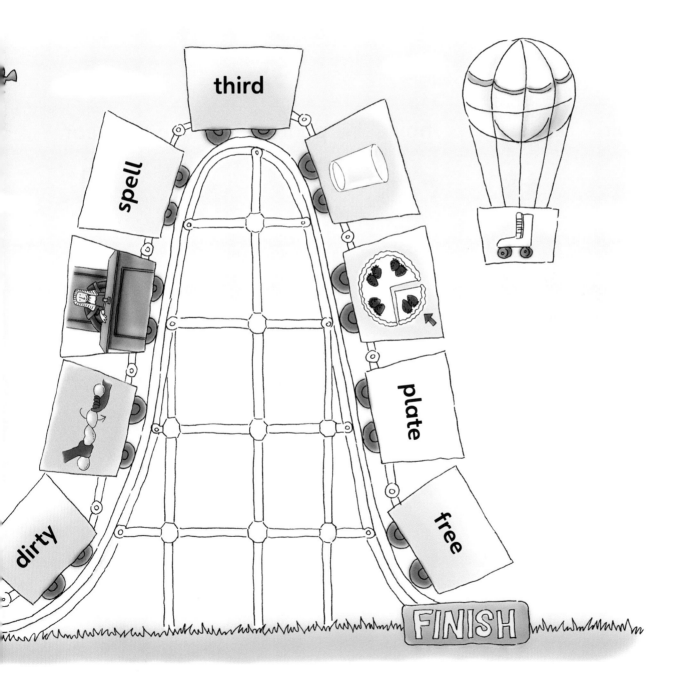

third

spell

plate

free

dirty

FINISH

ir
ear

bird	learn	shirt	search	thirty	early

air
ear

chair	bear	hair	pear	fair	wear

ear
eer

ear	engineer	near	cheer	year	deer

bl
pl

blanket	block	blue	plane	plate	planet

cl
gl
clean
climb
clock
glass
glue
glove

fl
sl
fly
floor
flower
sleep
slide
slow

br
pr
break
brown
branch
prize
price
practice

cr
fr
gr
crab
cry
fridge
fruit
grass
gravity

PHONICS DICTIONARY

 dr
 tr

draw	drink	drama	train	tram	tree

 sc
 sk

scarf	skate	score	skirt	scout	sky

 sm
 sn

small	smell	smooth	snake	snore	snow

 sp
 st

speak	spell	sports	stand	star	stop

 sw

swan	sweat	sweep	sweet	swim	swing

 tw

twelfth	twelve	twice	twins	twist	twenty

 qu

queen	quick	quiet	quiz	quarter	question

 c
 g
j

center	circle	cycle	bandage	judge	ginger

Pearson Education Limited
KAO TWO
KAO Park
Hockham Way
Harlow, Essex
CM17 9SR
England
and Associated Companies throughout the world.

english.com/englishcode

Authorized Licenced Edition from the English language edition, entitled Phonics Fun, 1st edition
published Pearson Education Asia Limited, Hong Kong and Longman Asia ELT © 2003.

This Edition © Pearson Education Limited 2021

First published 2021

Fifth impression 2024

ISBN: 978-1-292-32260-5

Set in Heinemann Roman 17/19pt

Printed in Slovakia by Neografia

Illustrated by Christos Skaltsas (Hyphen S.A.)